The EFFECTUAL PRAYER

A Beginning Guide To Prayer

Pastor Cynthia Thomas and Pastor Candace Kelly

The Effectual Prayer: A Beginning Guide to Prayer
by Pastor Cynthia Thomas and Pastor Candace Kelly

Copyright © 2023 by Cole Publishing
All rights reserved.
Printed and bound in the United States of America

Published by Cole Publishing
2023 Copyright by Candace Kelly and Cynthia Thomas

Library of Congress
Cataloging-in-Publication Data
ISBN: 979-8-9885825-2-6

Cole Publishing
4067 Hardwick Street #282
Lakewood, CA 90712
Email: ccpprod@aol.com

Book Cover Design by Covenant Images
For Book Orders:
Contact us at Cole Publishing Company

Cole Publishing

CONTENTS

SPECIAL THANKS

To the Father, The Son and the Holy Spirit for planting the seed and birth of this book for such a time as this. Father may You be exalted, revered and trusted by faith in every life that chooses this book of prayers. This book chose them because it is Your will for each person to have a close intimate connection with you. Thank you for hearing each of their prayers that you will answer according to your perfect Will for their lives.

I am also deeply thankful that you have given me a sister-beloved in Pastor Cynthia Thomas who exalts Your Holy name and is one that trust, revere and prays faithfully to You. Eternal One, I pray your riches blessings upon her life, her health, her body-temple, her peace, her purpose, her ministry, her leadership and her eternal joy. I pray not only for her, but also for her children and her children's children to prosper as their souls prosper. May the days of her life continue to be saturated with Your Shalom. In Jesus Name. Amen.

DEAR PRAY-ERS,

We pray that this collaboration of prayers will help you as you grow more intimately with your heavenly Father. We pray that the words on these pages will transform you and your prayer life as you daily assume the position of intercession that God has called each one of his children too.

It is our delight that you have chosen Effectual Pray-er as your prayer accompaniment.

This book also introduces you to the spiritual life as you embrace the spiritual disciplines that are designed to draw you into an effective intimate walk in Solitude, Community and Ministry.

Sincerely,

Pastor Cynthia Thomas and Pastor Candace Kelly

INTRODUCTION

"Prayer projects faith on God, and God on the world. Only God can move mountains, but faith and prayer move God. In His cursing of the fig tree our Lord demonstrated His power. Following that, He proceeded to declare that large powers were committed to faith and prayer, not in order to kill but to make alive, not to blast but to bless."

E.M. Bounds on Prayer

"... if My people who are called by My name will humble themselves, and pray and seek My face, and turn from their wicked ways, then I will hear from heaven, and will forgive their sin and heal their land. 15 Now My eyes will be open and My ears attentive to prayer made in this place."

2nd Chronicles 7:14-15 NKJV

"...The earnest (heartfelt, continued) prayer of a righteous man makes tremendous power available power dynamic in its working."

James 5:16 AMP

This powerful tool is to guide your daily conversations with the Father. He is waiting to hear from us as we anxiously call out to Him in prayer. Effective prayer will result in our application of the Word of God. God invites us to put him in remembrance of His Word.

Isaiah 43:26

God is so loving; He gives us His Word to give back to Him. He watches over it to perform it.

According to Germaine Copeland in her book "Prayers that avail much, she exhorts, "Prayer is this "living" Word in our mouths. Our mouths must speak forth faith, for faith is what pleases God." (Hebr. 11:6.) We hold His Word up to Him in prayer, and our Father sees Himself in His Word. It takes someone to pray, and God moves as we pray in faith, believing."

The good news is that His Word never returns to Him void because He watches over It to perform it.

SECTION I

Intimate Commitment

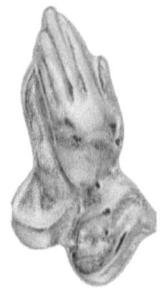

Prayer of Salvation

JOHN 3:16

For God so loved the world that He gave His only begotten son that who-soever believe on Him, shall not perish but come unto everlasting life.

JOHN 14:6

Jesus said to him, "I am the way, the truth, and the life. No one comes to the Father except through Me."

ROMANS 3:23

"for all have sinned and fall short of the glory of God."

ROMANS 10:9-10

that if you confess with your mouth the Lord Jesus and believe in your heart that God has raised Him from the dead, you will be saved. For with the heart one believes in righteousness, and with the mouth confession is made unto salvation.

2 CORINTHIANS 5:17

Therefore, if anyone is in Christ, he is a new creation; old things have passed away; behold, all things have become new.

Eternal God our Father, I am a sinner, and I repent of my sin. Thank you for sending your Son Jesus Christ to die for me. You said in your word if I confess with my mouth that Jesus is Lord and believe in my heart that You have raised Him from the dead, I shall be saved. Thank you for forgiving me of all my sin. I confess that I am a new creation in you, old things are passed away and now all things have become new in Jesus Name. Father, I open my heart to you, please grant me your Holy Spirit to teach me your ways and lead me in a righteous life pleasing unto you in Jesus Name, Amen.

Pray Often

I Thessalonians 5:16-18

Rejoice always, pray continually, give thanks in all circumstances; for this is God's will for you in Christ Jesus.

Acts 6:4

but we will give ourselves continually to prayer and to the ministry of the word."

Father, You gave us the example of Yourself, Luke 5:16 So He Himself *often* withdrew into the wilderness and prayed. And as you withdrew to pray, I withdraw from the daily pull of life and often go before you in prayer. That I may give you myself continually in prayer and to the ministry of the word.

As for me, I will call upon God, And the Lord shall save me. Psalms 55:17 "Evening and morning and at noon I will pray, and cry aloud, And He shall hear my voice."

And with every prayer and petition may I Thessalonians 5:16-18 "Rejoice always, [17] pray continually, [18] give thanks in all circumstances; for this is God's will for you in Christ Jesus. May the intimacy of my relationship be reflective of the time that is spent with you in prayer. In Jesus Name, Amen.

Pray Audibly

JEREMIAH 33:3

Call to Me, and I will answer you, and show you great and mighty things, which you do not know.

PSALMS 28:1

To You I will cry, O LORD my Rock:

Do not be silent to me, Lest, if You are silent to me,

I become like those who go down to the pit.

Father, because you said Call to Me, and I will answer you, and show you great and mighty things, which you do not know. I cry out to you daily in my prayers, making my praise, intercession and requests known unto you. To the people of Zion, you respond when I cry out for help. As soon as you hear, you will answer! To You I will cry, O Lord my Rock: Do not be silent to me, Lest, if You *are* silent to me, I become like those who go down to the pit. To the end that *my* glory may sing praise to You and not be silent. O LORD my God, I will give thanks to You forever. In Jesus Name, Amen.

Pray the Word

PSALMS 119:105

Your word is a lamp for my feet, a light on my path.

COLOSSIANS 3:16

Let the message of Christ dwell among you richly as you teach and admonish one another with all wisdom through psalms, hymns, and songs from the Spirit, singing to God with gratitude in your hearts.

Father God, your word is a lamp unto my feet, for the word of God *is* living and powerful, and sharper than any two-edged sword, piercing even to the division of soul and spirit, and of joints and marrow, and is a discerner of the thoughts and intent of the heart.

Lord, your word declares that heaven and earth shall pass away but your word shall stand for ever, so we pray Your word over all my life challenges and obstacles.

I cease not asking that you will fill me with the knowledge of His will through all the wisdom and understanding that the Spirit gives in Jesus Name.

May I effectively pray the word and worship you through all wisdom, psalms, hymns, and songs from the Spirit, singing to God with gratitude in my heart. In Jesus Name, Amen.

SECTION II

Transformational Prayers

Prayer for Heavenly Minded

COLOSSIANS 3:1-4

Since then, you have been raised with Christ, set your hearts on things above, where Christ is, seated at the right hand of God. Set your minds on things above, not on earthly things."

PHILIPPIANS 2:5-8

Let this mind be in you, which was also in Christ Jesus,

Loving Father, Wonderful Savior and Precious Holy Spirit, set my mind on heavenly things and help me to see from a heavenly perspective. Since I have been raised with Christ Jesus, I want to think about things that are above and not beneath, things that are lovely, true and honest, not deception, darkness and sinful. Thank you that You're teaching me to rule and reign with Jesus (Revelation 20:6). I pray that you would help me let this mind be in me that was also in Christ Jesus.

I am so glad that one day I will appear with Him in the sky. Prepare me for that day now. Develop the mindset of heaven in me and let this mind be in me that was also in Christ Jesus. I surrender to your righteous ways. In Jesus Name, Amen.

Prayer Armor

II Timothy 1:7

For God has not given us the spirit of fear but of love and of a sound mind.

Ephesians 6:10

Finally, be strong in the Lord and in his mighty power.

Lord God, I thank you that you have not given me a spirit of fear but of power, love and of a sound mind. I pray that you would shield me from harm. Cover me in your entire armor. I put on the helmet of salvation, the breastplate of righteousness, the belt of truth, the boots of peace, the shield of faith and the sword of the spirit. No weapons that are formed against me this day shall prosper and tongues that rise against me are condemned in the name of Jesus. Give me supernatural awareness in the spiritual realm. Be my eyes and ears Jesus and send forth your angelic army to fight on my behalf. Send the angels before me to clear the way. Let your angels fight against any demonic forces that may come against me today. Fill me with your courage and bravery. Impart wisdom and understanding. Show me the way that I should take in every decision that I make today. Be my rear guard. Protect my family. Provide for my family In Jesus Name! Amen. You are my refuge, my fortress, and my protection from all the dangers of life. I lay down all anxiety, fear, and concern. I put my trust in you, O God Most High. Help me to live and rest in you in this hour and always. Deliver us O God and rescue us from the hand of the enemy. In Jesus Name, Amen.

Prayer for Forgiveness

PSALMS 51:1

*Have mercy upon me God, according to Your loving kindness;
according to the multitude of your tender mercies.*

HEBREWS 8:12

I will forgive their wickedness and will remember their sins no more.

Lord, I come to you and confess my sin, wash me from my guilt and cleanse me of my sin. I acknowledge my offense. My sin is always before me. Please forgive me for what I have done to you. I humble myself before you in prayer in hopes that you will look at my mistakes and know that I didn't mean to hurt you. I know you know I'm not perfect. I know that what I did was wrong and not my best and I ask for you to have mercy on me according to your loving kindness, blot out all of my transgressions.

Lord strengthen me where I am weak and prone to fall. I humbly ask for a discerning ear and open heart to hear and feel what you are telling me to do. Lord, thank you for restoring me. In Jesus Name, Amen.

Prayer for Healing

PSALM 34:19-20

Many are the afflictions of the righteous, but the LORD delivers him out of them all. He keeps all his bones; not one of them is broken.

JEREMIAH 17:14

"Heal me, O LORD, and I shall be healed; save me, and I shall be saved: for thou art my praise.

Father, I confess my need for you today. You created me and you know everything about me from the time I get up to the time I lay down. There is nothing about me you don't know already. I humbly come to you today in need of your healing hand. I know that in you, all things are possible. You gave us life and life more abundantly. Please oh God, grant me the strength to move forward on the path you've laid out for me. Show me a path to better health and give me the wisdom to identify those you've placed around me to help me get better from doctors, referrals, herbalists, naturalists, and specialists. Please grant me peace and comfort during this time of recovery. I believe in the name of Jesus that I am healed according to 1 Peter 2:24 It is written in your word that Jesus himself took our infirmities and bore our sicknesses. Therefore, with great boldness and confidence I say on the authority of that written word that I am redeemed from the curse of sickness, and I refuse to tolerate its symptoms, In Jesus Name, Amen.

SECTION III

Prayers for Daily Living

Prayer for Employment

ROMANS 4:4 AMP

Now to a laborer, his wages are not credited as a favor or a gift, but as an obligation [something owed to him].

2 THESSALONIANS 3: 12-13 AMP

Now such people we command and exhort in the Lord Jesus Christ to settle down and work quietly and earn their own food and other necessities [supporting themselves instead of depending on the hospitality of others]. 13 And as for [the rest of] you, believers, do not grow tired or lose heart in doing good [but continue doing what is right without weakening].

Father I come before you seeking employment for your word declares, Owe nothing to anyone except to [b]love *and* seek the best for one another; for he who [unselfishly] loves his neighbor has fulfilled the [essence of the] law [relating to one's fellowman].

I pray for gainful employment that as a laborer, his wages are not credited as a favor *or* a gift, but as an obligation [something owed to him]. May I be a provider for my family, being self-sufficient in providing for the needs of my household in Jesus Name. Now such people, that are diligently seeking employment, we command and exhort in the Lord Jesus Christ to settle down *and* work quietly and earn their own food *and* other necessities [supporting themselves instead of depending on the hospitality of others]. [13] And as for [the rest of] you, [a]believers, do not grow tired *or* lose heart in doing good [but continue doing what is right without weakening. In Jesus Name, Amen.

Prayer for overcoming Fear and Worry

ROMANS 8:15

For you did not receive the spirit of bondage again to fear, but you received the Spirit of adoption by whom we cry out, "Abba, Father.

2 TIMOTHY 1:7

For God has not given us a spirit of fear, but of power and of love and of a sound mind.

Lord, you are my light and my salvation—Whom shall I fear? The LORD is the refuge *and* fortress of my life—Whom shall I dread? When the wicked came against me to eat up my flesh,

My adversaries and my enemies, they stumbled and fell. Though an army encamp against me, My heart will not fear, though war arises against me, Even in this I am confident.

Because of the promise of protection in your word, I shall not fear. Lord my confidence is in you for you have not given me a spirit of fear, but of power, and of love and of a sound mind in Jesus Name. I believe your word and trust your promises, therefore I will not fear what man shall try to do to me. I shall lie down at night and rest peacefully for I am victorious over fear and worry in Jesus Name, Amen.

Prayer for overcoming Mental Illness

PSALMS 56:13

For You have delivered my soul from death. Have You not kept my feet from falling, That I may walk before God. In the light of the living?

ROMANS 8:2

For the law of the Spirit of life in Christ Jesus has made me free rom the law of sin and death.

Because Jesus defeated principalities and powers and made a show of them openly, I stand against the forces of darkness that would come against my brother/sister in Jesus Name. They have been delivered from the power of darkness and translated into the Kingdom of your dear Son.

For You have delivered my soul from death. *Have You* not *kept* my feet from falling, that I may walk before God in the light of the living? For the law of the Spirit of life in Christ Jesus has made me free from the law of sin and death.

Father, in the Name of Jesus, I stand in the gap for my brother/sister until they come to their senses and escapes out of the pit and snare of the devil that has him/her captive. For your word says, Call upon Me in the day of trouble; I will deliver you, and you shall glorify Me."

In Jesus Name, Amen.

Prayer from Domestic Violence

JOHN 10:10

*The thief does not come except to steal, and to kill, and to destroy.
I have come that they may have life, and that they may have it
more abundantly.*

*Lord, your word is true and on the authority of Your Word,
The Spirit of the Lord is upon Me, Because He has anointed Me to preach
the gospel to the poor. He has sent Me to heal the brokenhearted,
To proclaim liberty to the captives. And recovery of sight to the blind,
To set at liberty those who are [b]oppressed.*

I pray for those that are oppressed by domestic violence in their households. I come lifting up males, females and innocent children up before you for You, oh Lord, are their deliverer. Because You have delivered us from the power of darkness and [a]conveyed *us* into the kingdom of the Son of His love, we are no longer held captive and victims of cruelty and hurt.

You are our safety and protection from the ruler of darkness for his tactics are exposed and my brother/sister is victorious because the thief does not come except to steal, and to kill, and to destroy. I have come to believe that they may have life, and that they may have *it* more abundantly. May my brothers/sisters dwell in a place of safety, peace and fulfillment, in Jesus Name, Amen.

Prayer for Healthy Nutrition

1st Corinthians 3:16

Don't you know that you yourselves are God's temple and that God's Spirit dwells in your midst? If anyone destroys God's temple, God will destroy that person; for God's temple is sacred, and you together are that temple.

Ephesians 5:29

After all, no one ever hated their own body, but they feed and care for their body, just as Christ does the church.

Eternal God, My Savior and my Help, I confess your Word over my body temple that reminds me that "no one has ever hated his own body, but feeds and cares for their body just as Christ does the Church, so Father, I ask that you help me to love my body in the same way that Christ loves the church. I have not always loved my body in this way. I have not always considered the consequences of my choices of nutrition. I repent that I have only sought those things that are mostly not healthy for my temple, like excessive sugar, salt, pork, bad carbs, fatty foods and drinks. Lord, I know I eat when I am depressed to feel happy, I eat when I am disappointed to feel good about myself and I eat when I am angry to feel joy. Food has replaced my dependence upon you to sustain my joy, confidence and peace. Then God, I eat all times of night when my body temple should be recovering and resting from the day. I know these habits shorten the quality of my life and can subject me to all manner of disease and challenges. So, I humbly come to you Holy Father and ask for your intervention. I no longer want to be driven by the lust of my flesh and lasciviousness and gluttony. Strengthen me where I am weak. Today, Loving Father I release my unhealthy habits and attitudes about my food intake and my body to You. I pray for the Holy Spirit to help me to honor You by nourishing my body well, seeing myself through Your eyes and trusting Your guidance and diet that is found in your Holy Word. So, by faith I confess my physical body is the temple of God and I commit to honoring it with better care by getting more rest, eating healthier foods and getting the exercise I need. I exalt you for the gift of health and I will make it a high priority in my daily living and remember to celebrate the gift of life as I offer my body temple as an act of worship to you daily. In Jesus Name. Amen.

SECTION IV

Special Relationships

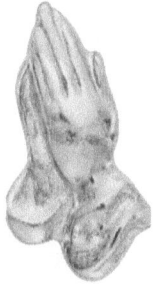

Prayer for family

1 Timothy 5:8

But if anyone does not provide for his relatives, and especially for members of his household, he has denied the faith and is worse than an unbeliever.

Psalm 127:3-5

Behold, children are a heritage from the Lord, the fruit of the womb a reward. Like arrows in the hand of a warrior are the children of one's youth. Blessed is the man who fills his quiver with them! He shall not be put to shame when he speaks with his enemies in the gate.

Eternal God Almighty, at times I find myself so worried about what the future holds for my family. Since COVID and other ills, we are struggling through so many different things. It's so easy to be overcome with fear and despair.

Help us Our God and Salvation. I know you promised us that you would be our Salvation and Strength. I pray that my family will trust in You and not be afraid of what comes our way. I declare and decree that we will rest in your promises for strength and salvation according to Isaiah 12:2 where you declare to your people, "Surely God is my salvation; I will trust and not be afraid." So God, let the love we share be a testament to Your grace and an example for others to follow. May our family bond be so strong that we stand united, no matter what life throws our way. In Jesus Name, Amen.

Prayer for Husbands

COLOSSIANS 3:19

Husbands, love your wives, and be not bitter against them.

EPHESIANS 5:25

Husbands, love your wives, even as Christ also loved the church, and gave himself for it.

Eternal God our Father, you are the perfect provider for us and you meet all of our needs spiritual and natural. Thank you for being our standard and our guide. I lift the husbands that are in my family line and pray for their strength that they would love their wives like Christ loves the church. I thank you by faith that they are couples of good report, that they are successful in everything they set their hands and hearts to do.

I thank you that they have obtained favor from you Oh Lord, and the will of God is done in their lives and in the lives of their family.

Then Father if there are any generational habits or patterns that have followed my family line. I pray against alcoholism, pornography, substance abuse, gambling and any kind of addictive behavior that exists. I bind it in Jesus Name and demand it loses its power. I thank you that my blood line shall walk in total freedom in Jesus Name! Amen.

Prayer for Wives

EPHESIANS 5:21-23

Submit to one another out of reverence for Christ.
Wives, submit yourselves to your own husbands as you do to the Lord.

PROVERBS 31:10

A wife of noble character who can find. She is worth far more than rubies.

L oving God I pray for wives in my family that they would respect and revere their husbands. I thank you that they open their hands to the poor and reach out to the needy. I thank you that their hearts are toward their family and their family has no wants or needs for anything that the wives/mothers in our family line, takes care to see about them. Her husband is known in the gates and the wife's children will rise up and call her blessed.

Father, I thank you that wives our godly, wise and grace-filled by your Spirit in Jesus Name and that they want for nothing. Father, I thank you that the wives in my bloodline are holy, righteous and godly examples for young women desiring marriage. Protect them and keep them and remind them that you are their reward in Jesus Name, Amen.

Prayer for Children

EXODUS 20:12

*Honor your father and your mother, that your days may be long
in the land that the Lord your God is giving you.*

PROVERBS 22:6

*Train up a child in the way he should go; even when he is old,
he will not depart from it.*

I pray for the children in my bloodline and their children's children that they would honor their parents with respect so that they may have a long life according to your Word. I also pray that wisdom would fill the hearts of each child and that they would be blessed with safe and godly friends and associations. Father, I pray against incidents, accidents, pandemics, endemics, and addictions as it relates to our children. I pray for their safety and that they would be covered by your blood.

Father, I pray against them becoming victimized by drug addiction, fentanyl, meth, crack cocaine, vaping, and any illegitimate substance that is against your righteousness. I pray against premature sexuality and the inordinate affections and soul ties that compromise our children's bodies in Jesus Name! Father, guide our children to choose the right friends even in unfriendly places, give them wisdom. In Jesus Name, Amen.

SECTION V

Special Ministries Beloved Church, Leaders and Outreach

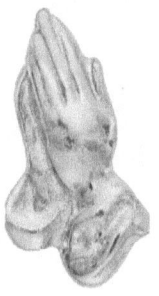

Prayer for Pastors

PHILIPPIANS 2:2

fulfill my joy by being like-minded, having the same love, being of one accord of one mind.

HEBREWS 13:17

Obey those who [a]rule over you, and be submissive, for they watch out for your souls, as those who must give account. Let them do so with joy and not with grief, for that would be unprofitable for you.

Father, I pray for my pastor, always in every prayer of mine making request for you all with joy, ⁵ for your fellowship in the gospel from the first day until now, ⁶ being confident of this very thing, that He who has begun a good work in you will complete *it* until the day of Jesus Christ; ⁷ just as it is right for me to think this of you all, because I have you in my heart, inasmuch as both in my chains and in the defense and confirmation of the gospel, you all are partakers with me of grace.

Lord, I thank you for their obedience in shepherding the local flock that you have assigned to them to oversee and that they will be joyful and diligent in the assignment that you have given them.

May the members abound in and demonstrate that they are filled with the fruits of righteousness which come through Jesus Christ, the

Anointed One, to the honor and praise of God – that Your glory may be both manifested and recognized. May they obey those who [a]rule over you, and be submissive, for they watch out for your souls, as those who must give account in Jesus Name, Amen.

Prayers for Ministers, Teachers and Lay Leaders

ROMANS 12:6-7

Having then gifts differing according to the grace that is given to us,
let us use them: *if prophecy,* let us prophesy *in proportion to our faith...*

2 CORINTHIANS 3:5-6

Not that we are sufficient of ourselves to think of anything as being from
ourselves, but our sufficiency is from God...

Heavenly Father, we pray for our Ministers, Teachers and Lay Leaders that they recognize that they assume greater accountability and are held to a higher standard with greater severity. We pray and believe that no weapon that is formed against them shall prosper and that any tongue that rises against them in judgment shall be shown to be in the wrong. My prayer is that You proper them abundantly, physically, spiritually, and financially.

We thank You that they will not offend in speech, saying the wrong things and that they may have fully developed character as mature men and women, each one able to control his/her own body and to curb his/her entire nature.

Having then gifts differing according to the grace that is given to us, *let us use them*: if prophecy, *let us prophesy* in proportion to our faith; or ministry, *let us use it* in *our* ministering; he who teaches, in teaching. Not that we are sufficient of ourselves to think of anything as *being* from ourselves, but our sufficiency is from God, who also made us sufficient as ministers of the new covenant, not of the letter but of the [a] Spirit; for the letter kills, but the Spirit gives life in Jesus Name, Amen.

Prayer for Imprisoned

PSALMS 91: 1-2,4

He who dwells in the secret place of the Most High
Shall abide under the shadow of the Almighty.

² I will say of the LORD, "He is my refuge and my fortress;

My God, in Him I will trust."

⁴ He shall cover you with His feathers,

And under His wings you shall take refuge;

His truth shall be your shield and [b]buckler.

I JOHN 1:9

If we confess our sins, He is faithful and just to forgive us our sins
and to cleanse us from all unrighteousness.

Lord God, thank you for hearing my prayer on behalf of the one incarcerated and imprisoned. May you be with him/her while they are imprisoned and thank you that you are with them in their time of trouble; Your word says that You deliver me and satisfy me with long life and show me your salvation. For if we confess our sins, He is faithful and just to forgive us *our* sins and to cleanse us from all unrighteousness.

He who dwells in the secret place of the Most High Shall abide under the shadow of the Almighty. I will say of the LORD, "*He is* my refuge and my fortress; My God, in Him I will trust. He shall cover you with His feathers, And under His wings you shall take refuge; His truth *shall be your* shield and buckler.

Prayer for Human Trafficking

JOHN 8:36

Therefore if the Son makes you free, you shall be free indeed.

ROMANS 8:15

For you did not receive the spirit of bondage again to fear, but you received the Spirit of adoption by whom we cry out, "Abba,[a] Father."

Father, I am free from the shackles of Human Trafficking through the fulfillment of Your Word that says, therefore if the Son makes you free, you shall be free indeed.

I am a new creation in Christ Jesus. Old things have passed away and behold, all things have become new. I therefore walk in newness of life as decreed in your word. I will praise You, for [a]I am fearfully *and* wonderfully made; Marvelous are Your works, and *that* my soul knows very well.

I will Trust in the Lord with all your heart,

And lean not on your own understanding;

⁶ In all your ways acknowledge Him,
and He shall [a]direct your paths.

For you did not receive the spirit of bondage again to fear, but you received the Spirit of adoption by whom we cry out, "Abba,[a]Father."

Father, by Your grace, I forgive my abuser/abusers and ask You to bring him/her to repentance in Jesus Name, Amen.

SECTION VI

Interpersonal Relationships

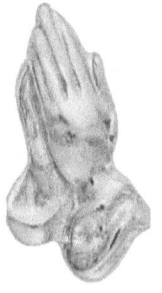

Prayers for Friendships

1 John 4:7

Dear friends, let us love one another, for love comes from God.

Ecclesiastes 4:9

Two are better than one, because they have a good return for their labor.

Gracious Father, teach me to love others the way you first loved me. As I build relationships with others, let them see you in the extent of my generosity, the authenticity of my kindness, and the depths of my love. And Lord, deliver me from ungodly friendships by force, in the name of Jesus. O Lord, connect me with friends, who are truly committed, in the name of Jesus

Loving Savior, please forgive me for not being the best version of myself in my actions towards my friend. Please help me find a way to show my friend how important she/he is to me. Please humble my heart to admit that I was wrong and ask him/her for forgiveness. Thank you for the gift of friendship. In Jesus Name, Amen.

Prayer for Single/Separated

PSALMS 37:4

Delight thyself also in the Lord: and he shall give thee
he desires of thine heart.

MATTHEW 6:33

But seek ye first the kingdom of God, and his righteousness;
and all these things shall be added unto you.

Righteous God, I take delight in You! In doing so, I know that You will give me my heart's desires! I am single right now and I understand that this doesn't guarantee that I will find a partner. But I have comfort in knowing that whether I am single or married, I can always find delight in who You are. Father, I adore You and I praise Your holy name with all that I am. Amen.

Wonderful Counselor, I pray that I seek first Your kingdom and Your righteousness, and all these things will be given to me as well. I pray that although I am single, I do not seek a partner more than I seek You. Lord, I have everything I need in You and I praise You for it. You are my Maker and my husband, Lord. Uniting with You is the only way that I can be truly whole. In Jesus Name, Amen.

Prayer for Widows

PSALMS 68:5

*A father of the fatherless, and a judge of the widows,
is God in his holy habitation.*

1 TIMOTHY 5:3-6

Honor widows that are widows indeed.

Lord Jesus Christ, we call upon Your blessed name and seek Your intercession as we lift up all widows in our prayers. Torn between their own lives and the responsibilities of family, may they in You ever abide. Strengthen them, Lord, in Your power and wisdom to lean on You and persevere in their calling.

Protector God, I pray for widows and orphans. I pray to lift them up, asking you to fulfill them, comfort them, and be a best friend to them. Use me to help, provide, and be an example to them. Give me opportunities to help anyone who feels down or less than.

Lord, I thank you for you have been my strength and hope, thank you my Lord, all glory to you, in the mighty name of Jesus Christ. Amen.

Prayer for Divorcees

EXODUS 14:14

The Lord will fight for you; you only need to be still.

MATTHEW 19:6-7

So they are no longer two, but one flesh. Therefore what God has joined together, let no one separate. Why then, they asked, did Moses command that a man give his wife a certificate of divorce and send her away?

O Lord my Healer, I need You to touch my mind, spirit, and soul and bring healing. My heart has been torn in two, and I feel like I can never heal from the betrayal I've experienced. And yet, I know all things are possible with You. In Your mercy and compassion, heal these hurts and wounds from this season of bitterness and pain. This divorce is more than I can bear.

I know Your Word says, "You hate divorce", and I repent for this action. Father, thank you for your mercy and grace. I am heartily sorry for my transgressions and my part in this breaking, please restore us to Yourself. Grant us and restore the joy of our salvation in You. May I taste joy once again as I rest in You. In Jesus Name, Amen.

SECTION VII

The Spiritual Life

In this section, we are inviting you to come with us on a familiar journey for many and quite unfamiliar for others.

Prepare yourselves to experience divine love, intimate encounters and a perfect companion, our Lord and Savior Jesus Christ.

I am confident that when you explore what lies beyond these pages, you will be drawn to a closer and deeper love and appreciation for God.

A Godly Woman's Prayer from Psalm 139:23-24

Investigate my life, O God,
find out Everything about me: Cross-examine
And test me, get a clear picture of
What I'm about: See for yourself
Whether I've done anything wrong-
Then guide me on the road to eternal Life.

Amen.

I n these two verses, the Psalmist reminds us to invite God in our space and place and measure us according to His mercies and grace. I invite you to try something that might be very unique to you.

Before you close your eyes each evening, engage in a spiritual reflection assignment.

Come to a quiet moment and space where you can invite God in: In your quietness, notice God's presence and loving gaze upon you.

Now ask the Holy Spirit to bring your day and your disposition throughout the day back to your remembrance.

I invite you to invest in a journal and to start your first reflection. As you reflect, using one-word descriptors, write those words in your journal.

At the end of your reflections and entering your descriptive words, pause and thank God for the godly distinctions you noticed throughout the day.

Next take a few more moments to pray for those areas of weakness as you confess them to God. Ask Him to strengthen you in those areas where you find opportunities for growth and transformation.

The next sacred vehicle that leads us to a deeper and more intimate walk with God is found in four easy steps stated by Thomas Keating, founder of the Contemplative Outreach Network that supports the practice of **Centering Prayer.**

Prayer is an interesting thing in that it is not the ultimate goal as some would think. Many of us actually miss the goal when we simply stop at prayer.

Prayer is bigger than the action of prayer. Peace suggests that prayer or prayer exercises are not an end in themselves; they are a means to an end. Nor is prayer even an end in itself. It, too, is a means. The end is contact with God.

Prayer is about being open to God. It is not about saying certain words in certain ways. It is not about feeling, thinking, or acting in a certain way.

Prayer is the word we use for the ways we open ourselves to the living God. Further he states, the problem in prayer is not with God. It is with us. Prayer is not a matter of waking up God or making God pay attention to us.

God's presence pervades the universe. And that presence is personal. God loves each of us all the time.

For Centering Prayer, you will need to be aware of four things:

1. Find a quiet place in your home, yard, car, school, chapel or park where you can be silent in God's presence for about 20 minutes.

2. Sit comfortably and with eyes closed, settle briefly and silently introduce the sacred word as the symbol of your consent to God's presence and action within. Be mindful of your breathing. As you inhale pray, "Lord Jesus Christ." As you exhale pray, "Have mercy."

3. When engaged with your thoughts, return, ever-so-gently to the sacred word.

4. At the end of the prayer period, remain in silence with eyes closed for a couple of minutes.

Again, this is not a means to an end itself, but it is an entrance into sacred time with God, the Father. Repeat this prayer practice at least once a day and you will be amazed at the transforming power it brings to your life.

Read: Matthew 6:5-6. Listen for what God is saying to you. What strikes you in this teaching of Jesus on prayer? Where and when can you be in secret communion with the Lover of your soul? Write in your journal about your experience in prayer. Pray for God's continued guidance.

Take the divine presence you have been given into the rest of your life. On the next page, feel free to record any reflections on your journal log.

SPIRITUALITY PRACTICES
AND JOURNAL EXERCISES

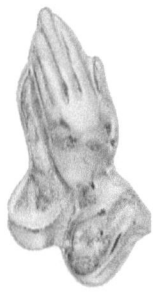

F inally, the Centering Prayer is not an intrusive and judgmental process.

It helps God's people pay attention to their life, to God's movement in their life and above all, enables us to hear what God's spirit is saying amidst the hustle and bustle of busy life.

In The Holy Longing: The Search For A Christian Spirituality Ronald Rolheiser says:

> "Spirituality is about creatively discipling the fiery energies that flow through us. Hence, a good spirituality requires a certain discipleship. A disciple is someone under a discipline. Jesus set out a certain discipline to creatively channel our energies, but He did more than this, and He was more than this."

If we're not careful, we will pervert the ministry of each other and the church by mis prioritizing what is important to Christ.

In the beautiful words of Henri Nouwen in _Compassion: A Reflection on the Christian Life_, he speaks of the Spiritual life and prayer in this way.

> "Spiritual life is life in the Spirit, or more accurately, the life of the spirit in us. It is this spiritual life that enables us to live with a new mind in a new time. He continues, "once we have understood this, the meaning of prayer becomes clear. It is the expression of the life of the Holy Spirit in us. Prayer is not what is done by us, but rather what is done by the Holy Spirit in us."

This no doubt requires discipline and consistency. Marjorie Thompson calls it a Rule of Life which is a pattern of spiritual disciplines that provides structure and direction for growth in holiness. She says,

> "When we speak of patterns in our life, we mean attitudes, behaviors, or elements that are routine, repeated, and regular. Ultimately the purpose of the rule is to help us grow into holiness. God calls us to be holy as God is holy, to grow into greater intimacy with the One we are created to resemble. "Beloved we are God's children now, what we will be has not yet been revealed. What we do know is this: when he is revealed, we will be like him, for we will see him as he is." (1st John 3:2)

These spiritual practices have made a substantial contribution in my character formation. I remain indebted to my Spirituality Professors at Fuller Theological Seminary who I have studied under:

Dr. Richard Peace, Dr. J. Alfred Smith, Dr. Paul Jensen, Dr. Wil Hernandez, Dr. Jude Tiersma-Watson, and the works of the late African American Mystic, Dr. Howard Thurman. Thank you for bridging the balance between Theology and Spirituality. We heed them both.

CO-AUTHOR

Pastor Cynthia Thomas has a heart and zeal for the kingdom of God. She desires to see the people of God, engaged, encouraged, and strengthen in His Word and living their best lives daily according to God's word. She has a passion for women, and she can be diligently found supporting women's ministry in her church and across various parachurch organizations.

She is a bible study teacher and prayer leader at Maranatha Community Church where she serves and is known as the Pastor of Prayer. She believes in the power of prayer and enjoys the intimacy that grows from daily conversations with the Father.

One of Pastor Cynthia's life verses is, "For it is God which worketh in you both to will and to do of his good pleasure."

She is a mother, grandmother, and great grandmother that resides in Southern California. She is a daughter of the King.

CO-AUTHOR

Rev. Dr. Candace Cole-Kelly is the Servant Leader at Acts Community Bible Church located in Long Beach, CA where she has served God's precious people for 20 years as their Senior Pastor. She is primarily responsible for nurturing and cultivating the Spiritual Formation of the Body of Christ where God called her to serve: Preaching and Teaching, Counseling, Vision Casting, Leadership Development, Outreach Ministry Assignments, Baptisms, Funerals and Marriages.

Preaching and Serving beyond the 4 Walls of the Church is her passion. She is passionate about women's ministry as President and Founder of Vessoul's of Transformation Sisters of Change to uplift and empower women's voices and advancement. God has used her gifts and light locally and around the globe and as far as Nairobi Kenya, Machakos, London, Germany to Middle schools in Long Beach CA as a guest reader for Read America.

Dr. Candace serves as a keynote speaker at Conferences, Universities, Churches, Prisons, and conventions.

Her social justice passion led her to work with the LAPD and Long Beach Human Traffic Task Force for years helping in developing strategies for abolishing Human Trafficking. She serves on various boards:

She is Co-Chair on the Executive Board of the Lakewood Interfaith Council. She is a Board Member of HumanSave (Human Trafficking Non-Profit Organization)

Dr. Kelly is Owner and Founder of Still Resilient International Training, LLC and Non-Profit Organization that provides evidence-based training through e-courses, workshops and conferences that are designed to address bias, inclusion, microaggressions and disparities. Her latest book is Nurturing Equity Minded Healthcare Providers (An Evidence-Based workbook designed to address Bias and Disparities). She is a prolific author of several books....and playwright of many musical stage productions. Finally, she is the owner and President of Cole Publishing.